# WHAT ARE AMPHIBIANS?, WHAT & WHY 1ST GRADE SCIENCE SERIES

BABY PROFESSOR

EDUCATION KIDS

Speedy Publishing LLC
40 E. Main St. #1156
Newark, DE 19711
www.speedypublishing.com

The word amphibian means two-lives. Amphibians spend their lives in the water and on land.

Amphibians usually have soft, moist skin that is protected by a slippery layer of mucus.

All amphibians
are
vertebrates,
which means
they have
a backbone
or spine.

Amphibians are cold-blooded, which means that they are the same temperature as the air or water around them.

Amphibians have adapted to live in a number of different habitats including streams, forests, meadows, bogs, swamps, ponds, rainforests, and lakes.

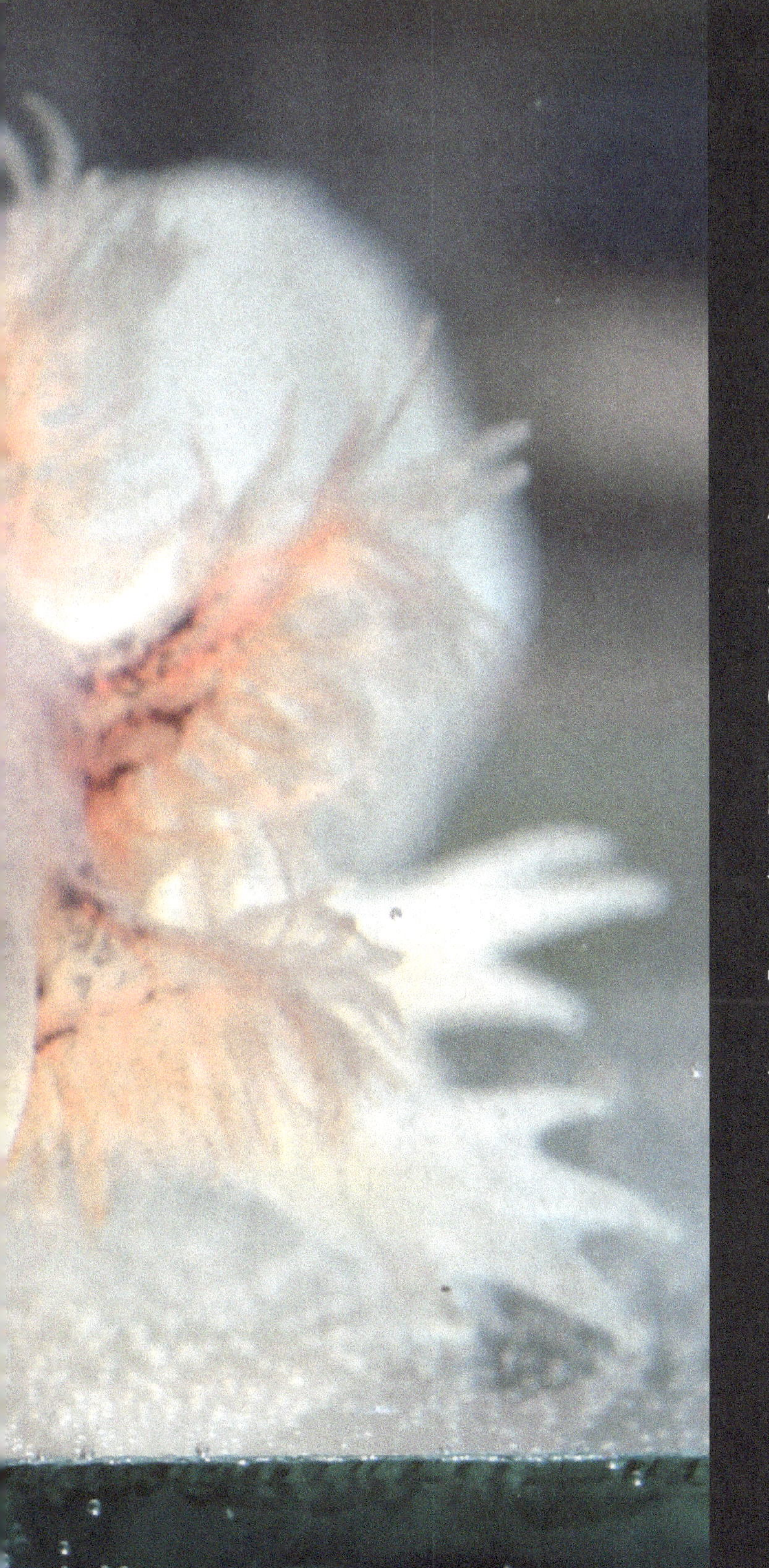

An Amphibian's skin absorbs air and water. This makes them very sensitive to air and water pollution.

Amphibians
are herbivores
as larvae and
carnivores as
adults. Once
they turned
into adults, they
will eat any
animal that is
small enough to
be swallowed
whole.

Amphibians have been around a long time. The earliest known amphibian fossil dates from 368 million years ago.